The Children

The Children

LUCY KIRKWOOD

THEATRE COMMUNICATIONS GROUP
NEW YORK
2017

The Children is copyright © 2016 by Lucy Kirkwood

The Children is published by Theatre Communications Group, Inc.,
520 Eighth Avenue, 24th Floor, New York, NY 10018-4156

This volume is published in arrangement with Nick Hern Books Limited,
The Glasshouse, 49a Goldhawk Road, London, W12 8QP

This publication is made possible in part by the New York State Council on the
Arts with the support of Governor Andrew Cuomo and the New York State
Legislature.

TCG books are exclusively distributed to the book trade by Consortium Book
Sales and Distribution.

A catalogue record for this book is available from the Library of Congress.

ISBN 978-1-55936-577-2 (paperback)

Cover image by Getty Images/Ian Tyas

First TCG Edition, September 2017
Third Printing, March 2020

Key

A forward slash (/) indicates an overlap in speech.

Words in brackets are spoken aloud but are incidental.

A comma on its own line (,) indicates a beat. A beat is shorter than a pause. It can also denote a shift in thought or energy.

The text has been punctuated to serve the music of the play, not grammatical convention. Dashes are used sparingly and generally indicate a hard interruption.

A Note on the Dance

In the Royal Court production we used 'Ain't It Funky Now' by James Brown, chosen by the actors from a shortlist, but I haven't specified this in the text as you could use anything. These are the things we liked about our track in case they help you in choosing yours:

1. It is of a period but not defined by that period. The play is not addressing a single generation, and it would be a shame if this moment made it feel like it was.

2. It is credible a group of friends might have choreographed a routine to it.

3. It is quite spare, so doesn't compete with the dialogue that is spoken over it.

4. It is cool. But not too cool.

This text went to press before the end of rehearsals and so may differ slightly from the play as performed.

Characters

ROSE
HAZEL
ROBIN

All in their sixties.

The light moves slowly from dark to light.
The effect of a painting being cleaned.
Revealed is:

A small cottage on the east coast.
A summer's evening.
The sound of the sea through the open door.
It is not usually lived in full time.
Camp has been made here by someone with a domestic hand.
Wild flowers in milk bottles.
Candles in wine bottles.
Tupperware fruit bowl.
The room is at a slight tilt.
The land beneath it is being eroded.
But this should not be obvious to the naked eye, and only
becomes apparent when, for example, something spherical is
placed on the kitchen table.

And ROSE.
Her nose is bleeding.
Blood has spilled down her top.
She looks around the room and does nothing to tend to her nose.
She looks for a long time at a basket of washing on the floor.
Finally she raises her voice.

ROSE. How are the children?

HAZEL (*off*). What? Oh, the – they're fine, they're – just keep
    holding it Rose! At the bridge. Are you doing it?

ROSE. Yes.

   HAZEL *enters with a towel.*

HAZEL. And put your head down!

   ROSE *puts her head down.*

   Here.

HAZEL *clamps the towel over* ROSE*'s nose.* ROSE *holds it there.*

I'm so sorry, Rose, it isn't broken is it? It's not swollen anyway.

ROSE. It's fine.

HAZEL. No I'm mortified. I don't know what – can I, sorry, let me just, I won't hurt you.

HAZEL *lifts* ROSE*'s chin.*
She gently wipes the blood from her nose and chin.
ROSE *watches her.*

Look at your lovely top. Would you like me to put it in to soak?

ROSE. No, / that's

HAZEL. Please let me, you can borrow / something

ROSE. No, I don't care, I hate it. It doesn't suit me any more. Honestly, I'll throw it away.

HAZEL. Oh you can't! Because of this? But I can get that out, no problem, I have a special, it's a stick, for oil-based products.

ROSE. Oil-based?

HAZEL. You know, blood, butter. All dairy really. Suncream. Semen.

ROSE. That's a big problem you have is it?

HAZEL. Well, when the boys were younger.

ROSE. You have boys?

HAZEL. Very young / I mean, not

ROSE. How many do you have?

HAZEL. What?

ROSE. How many / children?

HAZEL. Please let me wash it. It wouldn't take me ten minutes.

ROSE. It's fine, it doesn't

HAZEL. No but, I feel terrible, I don't know why I got so
    frightened, just / I thought I was alone

ROSE. I should have knocked.

HAZEL. I wasn't expecting anyone, we're so isolated here / so
    I just

ROSE. I did call out. The door was on the latch.

HAZEL. It isn't your fault. I've been on pins all day. And
    normally you hear the tyres, on the gravel so

ROSE. The taxi dropped me at the top / of the drive.

HAZEL. It isn't your fault it was just feeling you come up
    behind me, I sort of, I panicked.

ROSE. Fight or flight.

HAZEL. And also, (yes I spose) no but and also Rose, when
    I saw you standing there, Rose don't take this the wrong /
    way but

ROSE. It's fine, Hazel.

HAZEL. But we heard you'd died!

ROSE. Ah.

HAZEL. Yes so it was a bit of a shock.

    ,

    Lovely you're not of course.

    They laugh. HAZEL *takes off the apron she is wearing, shuts
    the door.*

    Sorry, let's – start again! So good to see you. Is it stopping?

    ROSE *takes the towel away from her face.*

ROSE. Yes, I think so.

HAZEL. Good, that's good. Sorry, what were you saying?

ROSE. Oh. How many children do you have?

HAZEL. Right yes, after Lauren you mean?

ROSE. Yes.

HAZEL. Three more

ROSE. Four children! God, / that's

HAZEL. another girl and, and two boys. Not children any more / of course.

ROSE. fantastic, no, of course. Because Lauren must be, what?

HAZEL. Thirty-eight.

ROSE. thirty-eight!

HAZEL. Thirty-nine at Christmas.

ROSE. Thirty-nine at Christmas.

HAZEL. A grown woman. Did you want to sit down, Rose?

ROSE. I just can't. I can't believe it. Thank you.

> ROSE *sits in a battered armchair.*
> *Without looking she reaches under it and pulls out*
> *a footstool, rests her feet on it.*
> HAZEL *watches her.*

She loved beards, didn't she?

HAZEL. What?

ROSE. Lauren. As a baby. She was cuckoo for beards.

HAZEL. I don't…

> HAZEL *takes a seat herself.*

ROSE. Because yes because every time she saw a man with a beard – d'you remember? She'd stick out her arms and scream with laughter

HAZEL. Well. She was a very friendly little thing at that age.

ROSE. and I spose Robin had one, didn't he?

HAZEL. Probably why she was drawn to them, / would you like some tea?

ROSE. I've always wondered about things like that, (thank you, love one) if there's a study or something, that charts our relationship to the things we're drawn to, as children, and how that changes as we grow up. I mean for instance does Lauren have a husband or partner?

HAZEL. Yes.

ROSE. Oh great. Great, no that's great. And so then does her husband or partner / have a

HAZEL. She's clean-shaven.

ROSE. She's clean-shaven is she? Well there you go, no correlation! I mean, an inverse correlation. Of course you'd have to test a much wider sample than just Lauren.

HAZEL. Rose.

ROSE. Yes?

Pause.

HAZEL. I'm growing a beard you know.

This morning – I found two hairs on my chin and I looked at them, for a good minute, and I tried to convince myself this was *alright*, it's natural, it's chemical, it's your age, you know?

She takes an apple from the fruit bowl, begins to polish it on her top or a tea towel.

Just oestrogen declining.

Because you know I don't hold with people our age trying to look twenty-two, because you see these women don't you, in the paper, looking like stretched eggs, trying to hide it when all it's doing is shouting it out loud isn't it, 'I'm old and I'm frightened of it!' I mean and because I'm *not* frightened of it so so so so but then I thought no. *No* because this is how it starts isn't it, the slow descent into the coffin it starts with two black hairs on your chin that you let run wild one day and you don't even know it but right there, in that moment, you've lost, you've lowered your defences and the enemy's *got in* hasn't it yes so I went at these hairs I went at them ruthlessly with a pair of tweezers and I can't describe to you the sense of triumph.

HAZEL puts the apple on the table.
It rolls down the table away from her.
ROSE catches the apple, returns it to the bowl.

ROSE. Grandchildren?

HAZEL. What?

ROSE. Do you have grandchildren?

Pause.

HAZEL. Oh. Yes. Yes, / Rose

ROSE. Hazel a granny that's insane! I can't / believe it!

HAZEL. Rose I'm sorry. I feel a bit. I might have a glass of water

ROSE. I'll get it.

HAZEL. No, it's fine, I'll –

ROSE finds a glass in the first cupboard she opens.
HAZEL watches her.

ROSE. I guess you're not using the tap?

HAZEL. No. There's clean water / in the

ROSE. Oh yes.

ROSE fills the glass from a large plastic container and gives her the water.
HAZEL takes it and looks at it for a beat before drinking.

How many?

HAZEL chokes slightly on her water.

Sorry, go ahead.

HAZEL *drinks*.
Puts the glass down.

How many grandchildren do you have?

HAZEL. Four now. Rachel has two and my sons have one each, they're poppets.

ROSE. I bet you're a wonderful granny.

HAZEL. Like it more than being a mother actually. I enjoy the feeling of handing them back!

The women laugh.

We haven't seen them since the disaster, of course.

ROSE. They weren't affected I hope?

HAZEL. Well we're all affected.

ROSE. No but they weren't, in the area or it's a terrible thought / I know

HAZEL. Well yes actually Rachel's lot were supposed to be visiting only by the time they got up here they'd closed the roads.

ROSE. So you were at home when / it

HAZEL. Yes.

Yes I was… making banana bread, for the children and, because it was the eggs, they started shaking in the box and – this sounds stupid, but I thought, they're hatching. Something's going to come out of them, like a, like a a

ROSE. Chicken.

HAZEL. No a Gremlin, but then because that's when I realised the whole kitchen was shaking, the plates started falling and the lights went out and the ground was sort of rolling and I thought this must be what it's like on a ship in a storm and then I thought, what are you doing you stupid woman, get out, just get out, so I did, I just ran outside in my apron, and

I saw the road cracked down the middle and then... and then it just stopped.

Pause.

ROSE. God. You must have / been

HAZEL. Yes so then I wanted to call Robin so I walked, I ran down to the beach, because the reception – and that's when I saw the tide had gone out. I mean it wasn't miles but it looked like miles, and then I saw the wave, only it didn't look like a wave, it looked like the sea was boiling milk and it just kept boiling and boiling and boiling and.

,

And then everyone was running, so I ran too.

,

I'm so sorry, did you say you wanted tea / or

ROSE. Lovely, thanks. Sorry it's so late in the day.

HAZEL *starts to make tea using hot water from a large thermos.*

HAZEL. Oh / don't be silly

ROSE. Only it took me a while to track you down.

HAZEL. Sorry I can't make you a fresh one. We're still on scheduled blackouts round here.

ROSE. I went to the house. Those lovely old pink walls. I thought – I heard you were still living there.

HAZEL. Yes but we left it, just after the disaster, we left it.

ROSE. But it's outside of the exclusion zone, isn't it?

HAZEL. Yes but only just, and we didn't feel like we could take the risk, I mean you can actually see it, the power station, from the house and the idea of it, I know that probably sounds, does that / sound?

ROSE. No, not at all. It's funny though isn't it. You think us, of all people.

HAZEL. You mean having spent so much time inside it?

ROSE. Yes you think, three scientific minds, we'd be a little more, insulated. From the hysteria.

HAZEL. No, exactly. I mean I'm not a silly sort of woman.

ROSE. No of course / you're not

HAZEL. But after. When we went back to the house, after the wave, after the explosions, I felt like, it's stupid but, I felt like I could *see* it the radiation hanging in the air a sort of a sort of filthy glitter suspended and I didn't like it, I'm not a silly woman and of course my background would suggest that I could but I couldn't I couldn't stand it any longer. Milk?

ROSE. (No thanks.) I would have done exactly the same thing.

HAZEL. It's skimmed.

ROSE. No, I really, I shouldn't

HAZEL. Are you intolerant?

ROSE. No.

HAZEL. No, sorry, none of my business is it.

> HAZEL *pours milk into her own tea and hands* ROSE *a cup of black tea.*
> ROSE *looks around the room.*

ROSE. It's a lovely cottage.

HAZEL. Yes, belongs to some distant cousin of Robin's. She offered it to us, kindly I thought because they're not close.

ROSE. But this place. It's only ten miles from the house, / it's not

HAZEL. No, it's just that little bit extra but it makes a world of difference to our peace of mind. And because the thought of leaving the area entirely felt somehow I don't know it felt disloyal, to the land if that makes sense?

ROSE. Well, you've lived here so long.

HAZEL. Yes exactly. I would've felt like a traitor. Besides, retired people are like nuclear power stations. We like to live by the sea.

They laugh.

ROSE. I nearly told the taxi to go off at the turning, it was like autopilot. Five minutes later I would've been walking through the car park expecting Ken to pop out of his booth to validate me!

They laugh.

HAZEL. Ken! I'd forgotten about *Ken*, I wonder what happened / to

ROSE. Dead I should think.

HAZEL. Oh I hope not, he was only young

ROSE. No I meant. If he was still... you know. Working there when the wave came and...

HAZEL. Oh. Yes. Of course.

,

You know lately I've realised it's sort of beautiful when the sun's on it.

ROSE. The power station?

HAZEL. Yes, when the smoke clears for a moment. That great white dome like a duck egg.

ROSE. I always thought it should have a flake sticking out of it.

HAZEL. A flake?

ROSE. A chocolate flake.

HAZEL. Oh, yes. And a drizzle of raspberry sauce maybe?

ROSE. making me hungry!

HAZEL. Sorry Rose, where are my, would you like something / to

ROSE. No I didn't / mean

HAZEL. No because have you had dinner? We haven't had ours yet. We've mostly been eating cold meals because the electricity doesn't come on till ten o'clock sometimes, and we try not to use more than we absolutely have to.

ROSE. Yes of course.

HAZEL. Salads because we're lucky this time of the year, you know, with the peas and the beans and the tomatoes. There's an old boy with an allotment up the road. It's been tested, it's perfectly alright.

ROSE. No well that's. Personally I find salad deeply depressing.

HAZEL. Well you just become aware of the risks, don't you. Osteoporosis strokes diabetes blood pressure, all the usual suspects –

ROSE. Cancer.

HAZEL. Well yes cancer naturally cancer! I do yoga you know.

ROSE. Do you?

HAZEL. I love it.

ROSE. Do you?

HAZEL. Absolutely love it.

ROSE. Really.

HAZEL. Oh yes. Fanatic.

ROSE. I'm awful with exercise. I get out of breath just looking at my sneakers.

HAZEL. Oh gosh, no we're the exact opposite, we like to keep healthy.

ROSE. I really admire that.

HAZEL *laughs*.

No I do, must take a lot of self-discipline. Of course it's easier when there are two of you isn't it, you sort of, cheer each other on, don't you.

HAZEL. I spose there is that.

ROSE. Whereas when you're on your own there's no one to slap the chocolate biscuit out of reach, so to speak.

Pause.

Move the steak frites from under you.

Pause.

Wrestle the sausage sandwich from your cold dead / hands.

HAZEL. We're not monks.

ROSE. No of course I was just, a regime like that, / you

HAZEL. It's not a regime.

ROSE. God no, I didn't mean to

HAZEL. It's just common sense isn't it? We've worked hard, all our lives, what's the use of all this time now if you can't enjoy it? If your body fails you –

ROSE. No you're right of course. I envy you.

HAZEL. When my mum and dad retired, they both sat down in their armchairs and never got up again. Drank a box of wine a night and watched TV from eleven in the morning.

ROSE. Sounds okay to me!

HAZEL. And they both lived well into their nineties like that – what? No, it wasn't okay it was death.

ROSE. But if it made them happy.

HAZEL. How can anybody consciously moving towards death, I mean by their own design, possibly be happy? People of our age have to resist – you *have* to resist, Rose.

ROSE. Hold back the tide.

HAZEL. You have a choice, don't you, exactly, at our age
which is that you slow down, melt into your slippers, start
ordering front-fastening bras out of Sunday supplements, or
you make a committed choice to keep moving you know
because you have to think: This is not the end of our lives
but a new and exciting chapter.

ROSE. That's a philosophy I really admire.

HAZEL. If you're not going to grow: don't live.

ROSE. Exactly.

HAZEL. No, I mean, if you're not going to grow, don't live.

Pause.

ROSE. Yes.

HAZEL. No, but you see what I'm saying, don't you? If you're
not going to / grow

ROSE. You've really got it all worked out, haven't you?

HAZEL. Well it's just what we think it's not rocket science.

ROSE *laughs.*

What?

ROSE. No, you just – I actually went out with a rocket scientist
for a while. In America, I used to try and trick him into using
that phrase. Like if he did housework or something, I'd
really go for it, what a WONDERFUL job you've done
mowing the grass, how DID you get this toilet so clean that
sort of thing.

HAZEL *smiles.*

What?

HAZEL. No it's. I'd forgotten what an odd sense of humour
you have.

,

ROSE. Right, well anyway, he never said it until finally one day, he made dinner and I went for it, how did you get the skin so crisp! And the inside so fluffy! And I moaned and stamped my feet and banged my fists on the table and finally the rocket scientist puts down his knife and fork, and he goes:

(*American accent.*) 'it's a baked potato, Rose. It's not brain surgery.'

ROSE *laughs hysterically.* HAZEL *laughs politely.*

People think we're a breed don't they? Scientists. They don't realise that we're all standing in different fields, just as in the dark about what goes on beyond our own hedgerows as the next man.

HAZEL. I met a geneticist once, at a wedding, and we were having quite a good chat about shrubs for a north-facing garden and then the dreaded you know, he says 'and what do *you* do?' So I said, I work at the power station, I'm a nuclear engineer. And he says, so what does that entail?

ROSE. God. Not really wedding talk is it, fission?

HAZEL. Exactly and so the heart sank a bit but I explained it, in layman's terms, I said well a slow-moving neutron is absorbed by a uranium 235 nucleus, and this turns it briefly into a uranium 236 nucleus and then that turns into fast-moving lighter elements.

ROSE. And releases three free neutrons.

HAZEL. And releases three free neutrons, yes, and he nodded and smiled and said oh yes I see but I knew he didn't, he was faking it, this… dumb show of comprehension.

I mean I could have said we use tiny hacksaws and a salad spinner, he wouldn't have blinked. And this is a man with two PhDs. So what happened?

ROSE. I'm sorry?

HAZEL. With the rocket scientist. Are you still?

ROSE. Oh no, no. We – it – it was

> a long time ago. He's married now. I'm godmother to one of
> their boys actually, well not godmother, more sort of non-
> denominational slush fund…

HAZEL. I'm sorry.

ROSE. God, I'm not. I never really fancied him properly, if I'm
honest. He smelt sort of feminine.

HAZEL. You've always been picky. All those poor men written
off for crimes they didn't know they'd committed.

ROSE. Yes but it's the small things that get under your skin,
isn't it?
Like there was this man I knew once.
And the way he lit a cigarette just took my breath away.
And he didn't even know he was doing it, but watching him
smoke, watching his hand hold a cigarette, made me want
him so much I had to cross my legs to stop myself going
down on my hands and knees to lick it.

> *Pause.*

HAZEL. In America was this?

ROSE. What?

HAZEL. Someone you knew in America?

ROSE. Oh. Yes, that's right. In… Massachusetts.

> *Pause.*

> He owned and ran a climbing wall.

> *A long pause.*

HAZEL. No, you're right, it's important to keep active. That's
why we took up the farm, of course.

ROSE. The farm.

HAZEL. Yes didn't you know? When we took early retirement,
we started an organic smallholding. We bought up some land

near the house. It was a lot of work, to get the accreditation, but you know Robin and me, we really threw ourselves into it. We won prizes for our dairy.

ROSE. Holy cow.

A tiny, disoriented pause.

HAZEL. Yes we're very proud of our / achievements.

ROSE. I'm sorry. I don't know why I said that, I feel a bit. Light-headed

HAZEL. Right, well would you like a glass of water?

ROSE. No. No I'm alright. Thank you. Sorry. Sorry.

ROSE *goes to* HAZEL, *puts her arms around her.* HAZEL *returns the gesture.*

It's so good to see you Hazel. I've missed you.

HAZEL. You too. You too.

They part.
During the following, HAZEL *produces salad leaves, tomatoes, pre-hard-boiled eggs, a bowl of cold new potatoes, tinned tuna, a jar of olives. She begins to prepare the salad.*

You come up, you know. In conversation, sometimes you come up.

ROSE. Where is Robin?

HAZEL. I didn't mean with Robin. With the others though, we're still in touch with most of them. We have a pub lunch every Christmas.

ROSE. But Robin's well, is he?

HAZEL. Oh, yes. He's out there now.

ROSE. Where?

HAZEL. On the farm. He visits every day.

ROSE. But the farm is – it's near the house?

HAZEL. Further down the coast

ROSE. But, so the farm is… inside the exclusion zone? – Isn't that / quite –

HAZEL. Robin is deeply attached to the cows.

,

ROSE. I see.

HAZEL. I'm deeply attached to them too. But I'm more attached to not getting cancer.

ROSE. But every day, / isn't he

HAZEL. Believe me, we have had this conversation, I promise you, that conversation has been had, but he's always been sentimental, you know that.

ROSE. So the house is okay?

HAZEL. No the house is a wreck.

We were lucky. When the wave came, the house was flooded but not destroyed. The fields and the garden were destroyed but the house was just stinking and full of silt it was cosmetic you know but I can't describe to you the stench. I waded through it up the stairs, the carpet squelching and something else, something dreadful, a smell a feeling a hopelessness. Like the infinite sadness.

ROSE. …

HAZEL. It's a film, the children used to, the never-ending whatsit you wouldn't know it.

HAZEL *gathers the salad leaves into a colander and washes them in container water.*

Anyway, I couldn't cope with thinking: how are we going to clear it up? and I cried, Rose, I just sank down at the bottom of the stairs where the pencil lines mark the children's heights and I / was just

ROSE. Your poor thing.

HAZEL. *crying* (thank you) because the mess the mess was just overwhelming

ROSE *takes the salad from her and shakes it dry.*

It was overwhelming Rose.

HAZEL *blows her nose.*

And then I had this amazing thought: we don't have to. We don't actually have to.

,

ROSE. Sorry, have to what?

HAZEL. To clear it up. It was like e equals m c squared, one of those exquisite pieces of thinking that's so simple, you feel like Archimedes running naked to the king, screaming 'eureka!' Because when I told Robin, the relief on his face.

And you know all our lives we've been those kind of people, when we have a picnic or, camping we don't just clear up our own litter, we go around and pick up other people's too, I have a little stash of plastic bags in my cagoule, that's just our policy, leave a place cleaner than you found it but but but so you see we'd *earned* it.

We'd earned the right, on this one occasion, just to say: at our time of life, we simply cannot deal with this shit.

And we decided to leave that night. And we went down to the barns and we fed the cows for the last time and I just wept, I honestly, to think what they'd been exposed to, their big brown eyes looking back at me but what choice did we have? They always say you shouldn't name them, but of course we'd named them, you can't not name them, so I'm leaning out of the taxi like a mad woman, 'Goodbye Daisy! Goodbye Bluebell! Goodbye Heisenberg!'

We drove away and we knew they'd all be dead in days.

ROSE. That must have been. Very hard.

HAZEL. Yes it was. It felt very. Final and that was, I found that quite frightening.

,

Yes but then a week later Robin decided to go back. One morning I woke up and he'd just gone. And do you know what he found?

The cows were still alive. All of them, flicking their tails and looking at him reproachfully! And that's when he decided he was going to carry on. He has to throw the milk away, but he goes down there every day now.

ROSE. Come hell or high water.

HAZEL. Well exactly.

,

ROSE. I still can't believe it's happened.

HAZEL. Yes well. It was a one-in-ten-million-years fault sequence. But this part of the country, we're basically in the same boat as Bangladesh, / so

ROSE. There is an inquiry.

HAZEL. Oh. And have they asked you to help with that? Is that why you're in the area?

ROSE. Oh, no. Not exactly, Douglas sends his love by the way.

HAZEL. Douglas Klein?

ROSE. Yes.

HAZEL. You still see Douglas do you? I thought he dropped off the radar. No, that's lovely. How is he? Send him our regards.

ROSE. I will. Perhaps you can yourself.

HAZEL *and* ROSE *look at each other.*
HAZEL *laughs. Goes back to preparing the salad.*

HAZEL. Yes, so that's us! A potted history, children, cows, la-di-da! I haven't even asked how you are, Rose.

ROSE. No!

HAZEL. How are you!

They laugh.

ROSE. Yes, fine, thank you.

HAZEL. No children?

ROSE. No.

HAZEL. Married?

ROSE. No.

HAZEL. Pets?

ROSE. No.

HAZEL. Oh well. You've kept your figure!

The sound of a car pulling up a gravel drive, off.
It is starting to grow dark, HAZEL *lights oil lamps.*

That'll be Robin. I think he'll be very pleased to see you.

ROSE. Do you?

HAZEL. Yes of course. Rose? Why have you come here?

Pause.

ROBIN *enters. He is carrying a child's trike.*

Darling look what the tide washed up!

ROBIN *stares at* ROSE. *He looks at* HAZEL.

ROBIN. Rose. It's not. Rose Cavendish.

ROSE. Hello Robin.

ROBIN. Rosie Dish, well don't just stand there! Give us
a squeeze!

They embrace. He gestures to the blood on her top.

(What happened there?)

ROSE. Nosebleed.

They embrace.

ROBIN. I can't believe it. How long has it been?

HAZEL. Thirty-eight years.

ROBIN. Yes because Lauren was just –

He looks at HAZEL.

Wasn't she, how was America?

ROSE. Yes.

ROBIN. You've not picked up the accent?

ROSE. No siree.

HAZEL. But you have. You say things like 'go ahead' and 'sure', you / never?

ROBIN. No, she always said things like that.

HAZEL. She didn't. I'd have remembered, Rose and I were good good friends, Robin.

ROBIN. Tell her, you have, you've always had a *twang*.

HAZEL. Sneakers. That's another / one.

ROSE. I suppose. I guess –

HAZEL. See. I guess.

ROSE. My dad and I used to watch a lot of Westerns when I was a kid and / so I mean

HAZEL. Kid!

ROSE. That was our thing, so maybe, I mean I've never thought about it / before so

HAZEL (*as John Wayne*). 'Get off your horse and drink your milk.'

Pause.

ROSE. Yes. That sort of –

HAZEL. 'Sorry don't get it done, dude.'

Pause.
ROBIN *looks at* HAZEL.

ROBIN. No other visitors today?

HAZEL *shakes her head.*

ROSE. Only me! Gave Hazel a hell of a fright actually. She thought I was dead!

ROBIN. Hazel's always doing that. Accusing perfectly alive people of being dead, I've warned her about it.

HAZEL. Didn't you hear that Robin? Last Christmas / maybe

ROBIN. I never heard that.

ROSE. By the way, how am I supposed to have gone? Something glamorous I hope? Rescuing a pram from a railway line or something?

HAZEL. No, I think they said, um. I think they said you were very ill, and that you'd got a little better –

ROSE. Oh good.

HAZEL. But then you'd killed yourself!

HAZEL *laughs.*
ROBIN *puts down the trike.*

ROBIN. Now then, you didn't kill yourself, did you Rosie?

ROSE. No, I don't think so.

ROBIN. You're quite sure?

ROSE. I'm pretty certain.

ROBIN. Well you say that but. Say 'ah'.

ROSE *sticks her tongue out and says 'ah'.*
ROBIN *puts his glasses on, examines her tongue.*

No, she seems alright to me. Dreadful halitosis, though.

ROSE *laughs, hits him, playful.*
ROBIN *laughs.*
Picks up the trike, shows it to HAZEL.

Rescued Zuzu's trike.

HAZEL. Well, I hope you washed it down.

ROBIN. Yep.

ROBIN *takes out a small Geiger counter and runs it over
the trike.*

Tell you what girls, you nearly lost me tonight.

HAZEL *tuts.* ROBIN *examines the reading.*

Nearly had to scrape me off the shingle.

HAZEL. Robin don't.

ROBIN. Twenty-five.

ROBIN *gives* HAZEL *a thumbs up, puts down the Geiger
counter.*
*He gets on the trike and, knees by his chin, rides it round
the table.*

It's a little game I play, Rose. The top field runs right along
the cliff and every year, I drive the tractor a little closer to
the edge and every year the edge comes a little closer to the
tractor.

HAZEL. The coast is just crumbling away around here. Has
been for centuries.

ROBIN. I tell you, it's a thrill.

HAZEL. It's reckless is what it is.

ROBIN. We're not dead yet my love. Our age, you have to
show no fear to Death, it's like bulls, you can't run away or
they'll charge. You've got to keep grabbing him by the
lapels, poking him in the eye and saying: not yet mate. I've
got your number, boyo. Keep him in line. Else he'll steal up
behind you while you're trying to get the lid off your Bingo
pen and have you away.

ROBIN *leaps off the trike*.
HAZEL *makes a 'there you go' gesture to* ROSE.

HAZEL. If you're not going to *grow*, don't *live*.

ROSE. Still. I really don't think you should do that Robin.

HAZEL. I've told him, he's mad, it's Russian roulette.

ROBIN. Only when I take a bottle of vodka along.

HAZEL *stares at him*.

Skol!

HAZEL *tuts*.

HAZEL. That's Scandinavian, there was a town, Rose, very
close to where we are now.
It was one of the most important towns in the country in the
Middle Ages.
Then one day it fell into the sea, the whole thing in one go.
The cliff just crumbled off like a lump of wet cake.
The houses, the school, the church, the marketplace.
Just tumbled into the water.

ROBIN. At certain times people say you can walk on the beach
and hear the church bells ringing from under the sea.

HAZEL. Crackpots say that.

ROBIN. She means locals

HAZEL. Well I've never heard it.

ROBIN. when she says crackpots, she means locals.

HAZEL. I am local. Lived here nearly all my adult life, I've
never heard it.

ROSE. I've heard it.

HAZEL. You haven't. It's nonsense. Ghost stories.

ROSE. I have. Very clear, at dusk. Ringing out for evening
prayers.

HAZEL. When have you heard it?

ROSE. In the summer.

HAZEL. You've been here, in the summer have you?

ROSE. Yes, of course, in the past

HAZEL. Oh in the past, I see, sorry, and that's when you heard these bells these ghost bells?

ROSE. Yes.

HAZEL. Well. You've always been religious.

ROSE *laughs*.

ROSE. Someone told me once, at a party, that out of every type of scientist, physicists are the most likely to believe in God.

HAZEL. Must have been a thrilling party.

ROBIN. Hazel's just jealous, we don't go to parties any more.

HAZEL. Well Robin drinks too much at parties, it's a liability.

ROBIN. Robin does, Robin drinks far too much, and Hazel doesn't drink nearly enough, speaking of which, have you offered Rose one?

HAZEL. I… yes I offered her a glass of water.

ROBIN. A glass of water! A glass of! A whole glass, did you, careful! She'll think we're rich as Croesus and nick our pension books when we're not looking.

ROSE. And we had tea.

HAZEL. And we / had tea, thank you.

ROBIN. Good thing you only come once every forty years Rose, you'd bankrupt us otherwise. With your demands for whole glasses of water. Let's have a drink. A proper one, to celebrate. I'll raid the cellar for something with a nose on it.

ROBIN *exits*.
HAZEL *smiles at* ROSE.

HAZEL. Robin makes wine. Elderberry. Gooseberry. If he offers you the parsnip it means he wants to get you drunk, it's absolute filth.

ROSE. I think, perhaps I should go. Come back in the morning.

HAZEL. If you really thought that, Rosie, you'd have already gone.

ROBIN *enters with a bottle and three glasses.*

ROBIN. I thought, given the occasion, we might crack open the parsnip.

ROSE. Lovely.

ROBIN *uncorks the wine.*
Pours it.
Gives ROSE *and* HAZEL *a glass each and takes one for himself.*

ROBIN. There's a smell comes off it at first but it's just the fermentation. It grows on you.

HAZEL. Literally.

They raise their glasses.

Are you hungry love?

ROBIN. Have we got any steak?

HAZEL. You know we haven't.

ROBIN. I feel like a steak. I feel like tearing something's flesh with my teeth

HAZEL. There's salad or crackers.

ROBIN. Salad *or* crackers! You mean I have *choices*! À la carte! Did you hear that Rose, the decadence coming from my wife's mouth, it's like the last days of Weimar Berlin in here tonight!

HAZEL. Not or, I didn't mean or, you can have both

ROBIN. Both? Both! Have you taken leave of your senses woman!

HAZEL. You're showing off, he's showing / off, Rose.

ROBIN *opens a box of crackers, eats two or three in one go.*

ROBIN. Can't wait until this is over I cannot actually wait to roast a chicken without feeling like the antichrist. How much longer do you think the power shortage will last Rose?

ROSE. Why should I know?

ROBIN. You're still in touch with the world. I imagine you as someone who reads a newspaper. Watches TV. Tweets, do you tweet Rose?

ROSE. I do not tweet.

ROBIN. No, we're not tweeters either, are we dear, we've barely mastered the microwave.

He picks cracker from his teeth.
Offstage, a phone rings.
ROBIN *and* HAZEL *look at one another.*

We're just simple retired nuclear engineers slash farmers who have no idea when the powers that be will resume normal service, get that will you Haze?

HAZEL *goes.*
ROBIN *picks cracker from his teeth.*

I've got a dry mouth now.

ROSE *fetches* ROBIN *a glass of water.*
The phone stops ringing.

ROSE. I don't expect it'll be much longer. A month maybe.

ROBIN. A month! Thank you.

ROSE. It's a good thing though, isn't it?

ROBIN (*downing the water*). What?

ROSE. Well. Learning to live with less.

ROBIN *picks up* ROSE's *hand and kisses it.*

ROBIN. But I don't want to live with less. It's hell.

ROSE. Well you might have to.

ROBIN *moves behind her.*

ROBIN. Well then I shall shoot myself with a bolt gun.

He kisses her neck.

ROSE. The resources are finite.

ROBIN. Well maybe people should be taught to use less of them then.

He buries his face in her hair.

ROSE. Well maybe you shouldn't have had four children then.

ROBIN *pulls away.*
Looks at the door.

ROBIN. You're upset. Because I never told you.

ROSE. I'm upset because it's fucking irresponsible but yes three more children might have been the sort of / thing you'd

ROBIN. When? One day a year, Rose, if that, when it suited *you*, when *you* deigned to – when one of those little notes arrived, nothing but a date and a time and an R with an order, be here, and I was, I was always here, I did, I dropped everything, always, I missed chiropodist appointments for you. Barbecues at the houses of solicitors. I stood them all up the second you landed on my doormat, and the reason I did that

ROSE. Such a martyr.

ROBIN. the reason I did that my darling

ROSE. I hate to think, what would've happened if I ever had / to compete with anything you actually cared about

ROBIN. the reason I did that was not to talk about my fucking children. Anyway you never asked.

ROSE. I asked about Lauren.

ROBIN. Because you didn't want to know really, did you, so don't be / so bloody theatrical now, especially when

ROSE. I always asked about Lauren.

ROBIN. Especially when I haven't heard a bloody thing from you for five bloody years, don't walk in here and start, anyway it balances out doesn't it?

ROSE. How does it balance out?

ROBIN. Because you don't have any. So if it makes you feel better, you could look at it like we just had your ration, and the balance books are still…

He mimes a pair of even scales.
ROSE *stares at him.*

ROSE. It doesn't make me feel better.

ROSE stands, turns away to the window.
Looks out at the sea. Tries not to cry.
ROBIN is surprised and alarmed.

ROBIN. I thought we were playing. I thought we were – talking in that way we talk where – we're horrible to each other but actually we're… flirting, Rosie, don't – I'm so sorry.

Rose.

He looks at the door.
Goes to her.
Touches her lightly on the arm.

Rosie.

ROSE turns, gives him a bright smile.

ROSE. What happened to your beard?

ROBIN. What happened to yours?

ROSE. Scared my students.

ROBIN. I had a freak accident during a tour of the Gillette factory. The doctors say it'll never grow back.

ROSE. I used to like your beard.

ROBIN. That was the main attraction, was it?

ROSE. Pretty much.

ROBIN. Scheiss. If only I'd known.

ROSE *laughs.*
ROBIN *throws his arms round her.*
She tries to keep him at arm's length.

ROSE. Don't. No don't. Please don't.

ROBIN *feels something different in her body.*

ROBIN. Rose?

She twists out of his arms.
But he grabs her hand.
He pulls her back.
He feels her chest.
Scientific, not sexual.

ROSE. It's not, I'm alright. It's, it was in America, the health
care's much better than here now. I'm clear. Eight months.
The left one was just a preventative… thing, Robin, don't.

ROBIN *steps away, very upset.*

ROBIN. Sorry. But you're… they got it and… you're… are
you, / you're?

ROSE. Oh, God, yeah.
No, I'm… It's just a nuisance.
None of my clothes hang right.
They gave me this special bra but it makes me feel like
a pantomime dame.

ROSE *forces a laugh.*

I'm sorry. I know how you feel about flat-chested women.

ROBIN. Don't be so fucking facetious.

HAZEL *comes back.*

Everything alright?

HAZEL. Yes.

HAZEL *assembles the salad.*

Oh, by the way. A man came today. Young. Clicky pen. He
said they're talking about putting those things those windmills
on the heath and did I want to sign a letter of support.

ROBIN *tops up their wine glasses.*

ROBIN. Well, wind. It's a start.

HAZEL. It's an area of outstanding natural beauty.

ROBIN. Only when you're there my love.

HAZEL. Creep.

ROBIN. When Hazel walks across the heath, the crickets all go cheep cheep cheep

HAZEL. Crickets don't cheep.

ROBIN. What do they do then?

HAZEL. They rub their hind legs together.

ROBIN. Perverts.

ROSE. Personally I think fusion is still our best hope.

ROBIN. Not after this.

ROSE. No, well. If no one loses their / heads

ROBIN. *It's a terrible thing.* A terrible dreadful thing, we can't just plough on as if nothing's, can we, no, we need more wine.

ROBIN *leaves the room.*
HAZEL *seasons the salad and puts it on the table.*
ROSE *watches her.*

ROSE. So the children are well are they?

HAZEL. Yes! I told you, they're all fine

ROSE. I think about Lauren a lot you know. Wondering, how she grew. What sort of life she has. Because when you've known someone as a baby, they're a blank slate, aren't they? The possibilities are infinite.

I mean, for example, what field did she go into?

HAZEL. What field?

ROSE. Her job.

Pause.
ROBIN *comes back in with a new bottle of wine.*
Registers the silence.

ROBIN. Okay who farted?

ROSE *laughs. Too loudly.*

HAZEL (*tuts*). Rose was asking what field Lauren went into.

ROBIN. Oh. Human / resources.

HAZEL. Human resources.

ROSE. Oh great. Great. She enjoys that does she?

ROBIN. She's on a bit of a break just now.

ROSE. Oh, great.

HAZEL. It's not great.

ROSE. No, I just meant. I really admire that generation, they're much more balanced than we were, don't you think Hazel? They understand work isn't everything.

HAZEL. I understood that.

ROSE. No, of course but –

HAZEL. I raised four children, I worked but I raised four children, they didn't suffer because I had a career, they all had costumes for Red Nose Day, home-made birthday cakes (hedgehogs, button moon) never had latchkeys till they were / teenagers

ROBIN. Hazel was a brilliant mother.

HAZEL. I'm not dead.

ROBIN. What?

HAZEL. Why are you using the past tense, I'm not dead.

ROBIN. No, I just / meant

HAZEL *starts tossing the salad with her hands, vigorously.*

HAZEL. I was very good with babies. I was in my element with babies, teenagers weren't my element but even there I made a good stab at it.

ROSE. I think I'd be the other way round.

HAZEL. No, people make heavy weather of babies but babies have a small set of very simple desires. They want food, they want sleep, they want to be clean and dry, they want to be held.

ROSE. I think that's all I want too, most days!

HAZEL. No, I expect there are all sorts of things you want that are much more complicated than that Rose! That's what I always liked about Douglas you know, he had very simple desires. He travelled lightly. I found him on the beach once at dusk with a sleeping bag and a Scotch egg, he looked like the happiest man in the world.

ROBIN. Douglas who, Douglas Klein?

HAZEL. Yes.

ROBIN. what are you talking about, he lived like a serial killer.

HAZEL. Which one?

ROBIN. I went round / there once

HAZEL. Which serial killer?

ROBIN. I don't know, all he had was two dirty mugs and a screwdriver.

HAZEL. Not Fred West, Fred West was a hoarder, Fred West had a vast collection of tools and he referred to all of them as 'she'.

ROBIN. Hazel's got very into murderers at the moment.

HAZEL. Lots of serial killers are hoarders actually, it's a classic sign. The accumulation of stuff is psychopathic. They have insatiable needs. More more more, that's what goes through the mind of a serial killer. Douglas isn't like that at all.

ROSE. And so Lauren is, taking some time off?

ROBIN. Lauren's had some problems.

HAZEL. Robin!

ROBIN. What? You didn't know her Rose, after she was a baby
but even as a child, even as a small child she had a / lot of

HAZEL. Robin!

ROBIN. rage.

HAZEL *slams plates down on the table.*

We used to call her the Vampire. It was very funny.

HAZEL. You don't know, she never went for you. Such sharp
little teeth.

ROBIN. Haze made her a little cloak. She was very fond of her
little cloak.

HAZEL. But mainly it was so you could hear her coming.

ROBIN. I never knew that.

HAZEL. It made a sort of swooshing sound you see.

ROSE. Sorry, what was wrong with her?

HAZEL. There's nothing wrong with her.

ROBIN. She's just quite angry.

ROSE. About what?

ROBIN. Oh. Everything.

ROBIN *takes* HAZEL*'s hand.*
HAZEL *smiles, grim, lifts* ROBIN*'s hand and kisses it.*

ROSE. Can I use your bathroom?

HAZEL. Do you want a wash?

ROSE. No, sorry. Your loo.

HAZEL. Oh, I'm so sorry! Just through there, the green door.

ROSE *goes out. Pause.*

ROBIN. Was that her on the phone?

HAZEL. Yes.

ROBIN. Did you answer it?

HAZEL. ...

ROBIN *sighs*.

ROBIN. Hazel.

HAZEL. She's left four messages today, it might have been an emergency.

ROBIN. It's never an emergency. What did she say? What did she want? Money?

HAZEL. No.

ROBIN. What then?

HAZEL. She was frightened.

ROBIN. Of what?

HAZEL. It was a sort of general terror.

ROBIN. Oh well, as long as there's nothing specific.

HAZEL *gets up*.
Fetches a loaf of bread and slices it.

HAZEL. It's funny, Rose coming, isn't it?

ROBIN. Not really. Nice to catch up.

HAZEL *tuts*.
Continues slicing the bread.
She slices the entire loaf.
Silence, until:

HAZEL. Oh by the way, I forgot to say, she got me a glass of water.

ROBIN. When?

HAZEL. I'd been out in the sun all afternoon and then I came indoors. I turned my back for a moment and suddenly she was just standing here, it scared me. Even after I realised... she's just got that sort of presence, hasn't she, like when the TV licence people come and even though you know you've got one you feel guilty, I couldn't stop talking, burbling on

about the hairs on my chin, I felt like I was going to faint or
something so I said I'm sorry, I better have a glass of water,
and she said I'll get it.

HAZEL *looks at* ROBIN.

She said I'll get it and she got up and she went straight to the
cupboard with the glasses in.

ROBIN. Well, she's like that, Rose. She likes to feel useful.

HAZEL. Yes, she went straight to the cupboard, where the
glasses are kept.

The sound of the toilet flushing, off.

ROBIN. What are you saying?

HAZEL. Me? Nothing, I'm just saying, she went straight to it.

ROBIN. And?

HAZEL. And nothing.

       ,

ROBIN. It's by the sink, that's where most people keep the /
glasses.

HAZEL. Is it?

ROBIN. Most people.

   ROSE *enters*.

HAZEL. Find it alright?

ROSE. Yes, thank you.

HAZEL. Rose? / Can I ask you?

ROBIN. Let's have a top-up.

   ROBIN *refills their glasses*.

ROSE. What?

HAZEL. I'm sorry, I hope you don't mind me asking / but

ROBIN. Hazel.

HAZEL. No, I should have said before but

well

did you do a number one or a number two?

,

Only the macerator on the downstairs toilet is very unreliable and if you did – if you did do a number two then it will cause it to overflow which is, it's a very messy / business so

ROSE. It was a number one.

HAZEL. so we only use downstairs for number ones, if you did want a number two I'd ask you to go upstairs.

ROSE. It was a number one.

HAZEL. Oh good! I'm sorry. I should have said before.

ROSE. It's fine.

> HAZEL *smiles*.
> ROSE *glances towards the door*.
> HAZEL *watches her. She almost says something. Doesn't.*
> ROBIN *shakes his head at* HAZEL, *warning*.
> HAZEL *looks at* ROSE.

HAZEL. I'm so sorry, I hate to / press the

ROBIN. Haze, drop it.

HAZEL. no but you're *certain* aren't you? Only I know it's embarrassing but it's better just to say now / otherwise

ROSE. I'm certain.

HAZEL. You did a number one?

ROSE. Yes.

HAZEL. Not a number two?

ROSE. No.

,

HAZEL. You know what I mean when I say number one and / number

ROSE. Yes.

HAZEL. Yes. No, good. Good! Sorry. That's wonderful.

ROBIN. Jesus.

HAZEL. What? Don't, looking at me like that, it's not you
who'd be on their knees with a J-cloth cleaning / up her

ROBIN. Hazel!

HAZEL. God, you're so squeamish darling! Rose doesn't mind!
It's a perfectly natural bodily function! He's always been like
this, even with four tiny babies, wonderful father so long as
nothing was leaking out of them!

ROBIN. That's rubbish. That's, you know / that's

HAZEL. Is it? Oh I'm so sorry, I must have remembered my
entire life wrong.

*HAZEL coolly picks up the wind-up radio and starts
winding it up.*
ROBIN watches her for a moment or two.

ROBIN. Do you have to do that now?

HAZEL. This is when I wind it. If I don't wind it now then
I can't listen to Radio 4 in the morning.

*She continues to wind. Pause. ROBIN tries to tolerate it.
Fails.*

ROBIN. It's just it's, it's really / irritating

HAZEL. I heard another man died today.

ROSE. From the plant?

HAZEL. There are cats and dogs running wild around it,
apparently. No one to stop them, and how are they supposed
to know? What they're breathing in, it breaks my heart.

ROBIN. Hazel's soppy about animals. I once said to Hazel,
what would upset you more, to see a car hit a dog, or a child?

HAZEL. Robin. (*To* ROSE.) Don't listen to him, he embroiders.

ROSE. What did she say?

ROBIN. She said 'a nice child or a nasty one?'

HAZEL. That was a joke, you know that / was a

ROBIN. No, she said the child.

HAZEL. Of course I said the child!

ROBIN. Yes of course, she said the child. Eventually.

HAZEL. Eventually what does that mean eventually?

ROBIN. It means my love you had to *think about it*.

HAZEL. I did not.

ROBIN. For at least a minute.

HAZEL. A minute!

ROBIN. It was it was nearly exactly a minute.

HAZEL. Were you counting then I didn't notice you counting

ROBIN. No

HAZEL. Didn't notice your lips moving

ROBIN. I wasn't counting

HAZEL. Did you have some sort of mental stop/watch

ROBIN. No

HAZEL. Well then how could you know it was / a minute

ROBIN. BECAUSE I WAS BOILING AN EGG AT THE TIME.

,

HAZEL *stops winding the radio. Puts it down.*

HAZEL. You should have had an elderberry. The parsnip always makes you belligerent.

ROBIN. Yes well that's my prerogative. As an old man that's / my prerogative

HAZEL. 'Old', you're not old.

ROBIN. Young men get impotent rage, old men get incontinent belligerence.

ROSE. And what do old women get then?

ROBIN. Fat.

He downs his glass, pours another.

Present company excepted.

HAZEL. Oh well that's nice. Is this what you were expecting Rose? To drop by on some old friends and be told you're old and fat?

ROSE. You look amazing Hazel, I don't know how / you

ROBIN. She drinks the blood of virgins.

HAZEL. It's just good diet and exercise.

ROBIN. Oh yes. That's what I meant. Good diet and exercise. Not the blood of virgins. Hazel doesn't need the blood of virgins. Hazel does yoga.

ROSE. I know.

ROBIN *refills their glasses.*

ROBIN. Oh you know do you? Yes, she's very bendy. She could pick her nose with her toes if she wanted.

HAZEL. How do you know I don't?

ROBIN. Because I watch you. When you roll out your mat I watch you and I say a prayer a special prayer that I made up in my head just for you, it goes like this:

'The earth may be irradiated
The seas may rise up and wash us away
The human race may eat itself
But may Hazel's sun always be saluted
And her dog always be downward!'

He toasts her. She looks at him. Pause.

HAZEL. That's nice, dear.

ROBIN. Nice? Nice! Hazel saved my life. If I wasn't married to Hazel, the walls of my arteries would look like loft insulation. Together Hazel and I are going to live forever. On a diet of yoga and yogurt.

ROBIN kisses HAZEL.
HAZEL pulls away.

HAZEL. Well it's in my interests isn't it.

ROBIN. Oh stop! No romance please, not in front of the guest.

HAZEL. Rose isn't a guest, Rose is an old old friend.

ROBIN. Oi now! Less of the old! Rose doesn't look a day over eighty.

ROSE. Fuck off Robin.

ROBIN stares at her.
Then laughs.
Raises his glass to her.

ROBIN. Yes, exactly. 'Fuck off Robin.'

ROBIN sits.
Pause.

(*To* HAZEL.) Come here. Sit on my lap.

HAZEL. Sit on your? Good grief, Robin.

ROBIN. What?

HAZEL lets out a very long sigh.

HAZEL. Just because you and Rose once went to bed a few times you assume the only reason she could have come here tonight is to steal you away from me and so, sweetly but very misguidedly, you're smothering me in affection. And it's so transparent, it's embarrassing, darling.

Pause.

ROBIN. My mistake. I'm sorry Rose. My middle-aged spread has gone entirely to my ego.

HAZEL. You remember, he's just like this sometimes, it's harmless, it only comes of liking women. We used to have a girl to do the milking

ROBIN (*sings the name*). Fiooooooooona!

HAZEL. Fiona, yes, she came to do the milking / and

ROBIN. Fiona. With two Fs.

> ROBIN *makes a gesture to signify enormous tits.*
> *Halfway through he finds* ROSE *looking at him and he*
> *falters, mortified.*

HAZEL. You couldn't take your eyes off them. Even I couldn't, to be fair, they were mesmerising. In the end I had to take her aside and suggest that, for the more manual work, she might like to start wearing a bra.

> ROSE *takes out her cigarettes.*
> ROBIN *recovers himself.*

ROBIN. I knew you'd put the wind up her.

HAZEL. Well, she was estranged from her mother, wasn't she, she didn't have anyone to tell her, so I said to her, it's all very well now when the skin is elastic, but you'll thank me in twenty years when they're not down by your knees.

ROBIN. Killjoy.

HAZEL. Perv.

ROBIN. Puritan

HAZEL. Lech.

ROBIN. Jealous old bitch.

HAZEL. Dirty old man.

> ROBIN *raises his glass.*

ROBIN. Cheers.

HAZEL. Cheers!

ROBIN. To Fiona.

HAZEL. And all who sail in her!

> ROBIN *and* HAZEL *laugh and clink glasses.*
> HAZEL *sits on* ROBIN's *lap.*
> *He pats her arse fondly.*
> *Pause.*

ROSE. Do you mind?

> ROSE *is holding up her cigarettes.*

HAZEL. Oh, yes – would you mind standing at the door?

ROBIN. Are you sure that's a good idea?

HAZEL. She's a grown woman, she can dig her own grave, it's fine Rose.

> ROSE *moves her chair to the back door.*
> *Opens it and sits, lights a cigarette. Smokes.*
> *The sound of the sea from the dark outside.*
> ROBIN *watches* ROSE.

ROBIN. So you didn't come to seduce me, then?

ROSE. 'Fraid not.

ROBIN. You're certain? You don't want to think about it?

ROSE. No, I'm quite sure. Hang on… yep, no. Wouldn't touch you with a bargepole. You've aged very badly Robin.

> ROBIN *groans, mimes shooting himself in the head.*
> HAZEL *pats him on the head.*

HAZEL. Poor love. Not fair is it, men are supposed to grow into their looks, aren't they, it's the women who go to seed.

ROSE. Whereas Robin's got a face like a haunted house.

> *The women start to laugh.*

ROBIN. Oh that's nice. That's charming.

HAZEL. Don't worry. I can still tolerate looking at you, darling. If I squint.

> *She squints. The women laugh harder.*

ROBIN. You're very funny, both of you.

The women laugh harder.

You both have a winning sense of humour.

The women laugh harder.

Which is lucky given you're both such fat old hags.

The women laugh hysterically.

But it does beg the question though, doesn't it? If you've not come here tonight to woo me away from Hazel, then why have you come?

ROSE *takes a drag on her cigarette.*

ROSE. I'm going back. To work at the power station.

,

HAZEL. You're not serious.

ROSE. Yes.

ROSE *laughs.*

I mean. Yes. Somebody has to restore control.

HAZEL *gets up from* ROBIN.

ROBIN. Rose, are you sure / you want to

HAZEL. There are people doing that.

ROSE. Yes of course, but they're all so young. Most of the engineers are under thirty-five / and

ROBIN. But it's their job. It's what they're trained for.

ROSE. Yes and but lots of them have families. Their whole lives ahead, and I just feel, I feel very strongly. It's not fair. Every day they're there is less life. They've raised the radiation exposure limit from a hundred millisieverts to two hundred and fifty / millisieverts

ROBIN. Yes we heard.

ROSE. These… *young people* these *children*, basically, actually
    with their whole lives ahead and it's not fair it's not right it
    seems *wrong*. Doesn't it? Because we built it, didn't we? Or
    helped to, we're responsible, so I do, I feel the need to, to to

HAZEL. To clear it up.

ROSE. Yes. Yes.

Pause.
ROSE *finishes her cigarette, closes the door.*

ROBIN. That's…

HAZEL. That's very brave.

ROSE. Brave?

HAZEL. Yes, brave, very brave very, I don't know

ROBIN. Noble.

ROSE. I don't think I'm particularly special.

HAZEL. Don't you?

ROSE. No. I think most people would, if they could, if they had
    the education, the expertise, the knowledge / that we

HAZEL. But then you don't have any children

ROSE. No I suppose not

HAZEL. grandchildren

ROSE. No but

HAZEL. you're not married.

ROBIN. Shut up Hazel.

HAZEL. I'm sorry?

ROBIN. Just fucking shut up for a fucking minute will you?

    ROBIN *takes* ROSE*'s hands.*

    It's death, Rose. You understand that?

    HAZEL *takes out a can of air freshener from under the sink
    and sprays it liberally.*

HAZEL. Of course she understands it, she's a leader in her field.

ROBIN. They're playing it down in the press, to protect the industry –

HAZEL. Of course they are, they / have to

ROBIN. That's not what / I'm

HAZEL. No good getting silly about nuclear because what's the alternative?

ROBIN. Whose idea was it? Who asked you to do this?

ROSE. No one. It was my idea. When I heard about the wave, and the meltdown, when I saw it on the news, and understood the full, the mess, the meaning of this, the thought came into my head immediately. And of course I dismissed it but I couldn't shake it off…

(*To* HAZEL.) It was like you with the house after the wave. It was so simple. Like Archimedes, I knew it was right.

Right now I'm looking for a team of twenty people over the age of sixty-five. To take over and let the young ones go, while they still have the chance, while there's still the possibility of, well, life.

I still have contacts at the Science Council so I flew back and I took it to them and they, I think fast-tracked is the word and, so what happened is I've been in talks with the Government, and the operating company and two weeks ago they approved the proposal. So now I've been… gathering people.

HAZEL. People.

ROSE. Yes, we're going to need scientists, engineers. Construction workers, that's not my field, I'm leaving that to Mike Briar.

The last few weeks I've been writing emails, making phone calls but mostly going about the country, visiting people

HAZEL. Guilt-tripping them.

ROSE. No I don't think all of them saw it like that.

HAZEL. Oh, didn't they? That's good.

ROSE. No, I think a lot of them were, not happy, but, relieved maybe. I think there was relief, that someone was taking charge.

,

HAZEL. Horse shit.

ROBIN. Hazel.

HAZEL. No, I'm sorry but horse shit horse *shit*! that's not / how they felt

ROBIN. How many have you asked?

ROSE. Well it's… maybe about a hundred / or

ROBIN. And these other people have agreed to, to do this?

ROSE. Yes. Well, no only eighteen so far, / but

HAZEL. Eighteen?

ROBIN. Anyone we know?

ROSE. One or two.

ROBIN. Not Douglas.

ROSE. Actually Douglas was among the first.

ROBIN. No, not Douglas.

> HAZEL *starts putting out cutlery, plates.*

HAZEL. Why not Douglas? Douglas was a brilliant man, and very brave. Don't you remember, he offered to give his cousin his kidney?

ROBIN. He didn't actually give it though did he?

HAZEL. No because the cousin fell off a viaduct unfortunately.

ROBIN. And I'll bet old Douglas breathed a sigh of relief!

HAZEL. It isn't the point whether he breathed a sigh of relief the point is he would have given it, the point is he offered, isn't that right Rose?

ROSE. Well, you can function perfectly well with only one, can't you?

HAZEL. Yes but why would you want to? Are you eating Rose? It's only salad and bread but you're welcome.

ROSE. Thank you.

HAZEL *clatters a plate and cutlery down before* ROSE.

ROBIN. So. So when are you going?

ROSE. Tonight.

ROBIN. Tonight?

ROSE. The others are on their way. I thought I'd have more time, but… this morning there was a radiation spike. They should be pulling them all out but they can't, there are major leaks in unit two, somehow there's contaminated water flooding into the discharge channel.

ROBIN *groans in horror.*

HAZEL. Oh God.

ROBIN. And so how long have you got?

ROSE. You mean –

ROBIN. Before it starts spilling into the sea.

ROSE. Oh. About three feet.

ROBIN. Right. Right.

,

ROSE. Yes so we'll be taking over from the skeleton crew first thing in the morning.

ROBIN. And you're telling us this because…?

HAZEL. Don't be callow Robin.

You understand perfectly well what she's saying what she's asking / well I'm sorry but no

ROBIN. No but is that what you're saying? Are you asking / us to

ROSE. I'd like you to consider it.

HAZEL. It's out of the question. Help yourself to salad.

ROSE. Both of you worked at the power station for a long time. Much longer than me and –

HAZEL. Not for years.

HAZEL *starts to shake the dressing.*

ROBIN. And is twenty enough / to

HAZEL. Eighteen.

ROBIN. What?

HAZEL. She's only got eighteen. Dressing?

ROSE. Twenty's just (no, thank you), twenty's just to start with. We're going to need more of course, lots more, hundreds, but if we can get enough, we can let most of the young ones go and still reach a cold shut-down by Christmas. But I'm out of touch. The people I've been contacting, I haven't seen most of them for thirty years. Some of them don't even remember me.

HAZEL. Don't be silly, you're a very memorable person, I expect they were just trying to get rid of you.

ROSE. But you're still in contact with so many of them, people like you, people always liked you. I was hoping you might be open to, helping / me to

HAZEL. Oh this gets better and better, you want us to recruit for you? Is that what you're, ding dong can I talk to you about Jesus?

ROSE. I think if people knew you were there it would inspire confidence.

HAZEL. I'm sure it would.

ROSE. I think it would make them feel safe.

ROBIN. But it's not safe, in fact it's very unsafe, they're not stupid Rose.

ROSE. Yes but

HAZEL. Yes but what?

ROSE. You have the power to… you have a power. You have power, and you've both already had long and full lives.

HAZEL. Long? Long, I'm sixty-seven that's / not *long*

ROSE. The people working there now are in their twenties and thirties, they have young families, / it's not

HAZEL. Look it's, what you don't – is I come from a line of very long-living women. My granny was a hundred and three when she died peacefully in her sleep, not bleeding from her gums not hair falling out nausea bloody vomit diarrhoea not leukaemia, / body riddled with

ROSE. The effects of the radiation could take twenty years to affect us by which time we'll be –

HAZEL. By which time we'll be dead anyway?

ROSE. Probably, yes. Or dying.

HAZEL. I AM NOT OLD.

ROBIN. You must have known, what you're saying, what you're / asking

HAZEL. She is saying you are past your sell-by date, you are dispensable, shrivelled-up cannon fodder, this bloody COUNTRY. I should've lived in the Mediterranean! I could have sat under an olive grove until I was a hundred and twenty like a pickled walnut, I would've been respected, they would have called me Gerondissa, my age would have been a badge a badge of honour, / not

ROSE. I think there is honour in this. I think this is very / honourable

HAZEL. How dare you come here. Show up unannounced and bring, bringing this / poison into our

ROSE. I did send an email.

HAZEL. What good is that when we aren't using the computer?

ROBIN. No, we're not using the computer Rose, it eats up the power.

HAZEL. And anyway what a thing to write in an email 'dear robin and hazel how are you I am well would you like to come and get cancer with me?' What font / did you use?

ROBIN. Hazel, please.

HAZEL. Did you put a little smiley face at the end? A row of kisses? LOL RSVP?

ROSE. It was more. General.

HAZEL starts to serve the salad.

HAZEL. And what I resent most is is is is is your tone your expectation that we will feel *guilty*. What am I supposed to feel guilty about? I've done my bit. I I I I I I I / I

ROBIN. You helped them remove the topsoil from the playground didn't you?

HAZEL. I did, I helped them do that.

ROBIN. And we barely use any power.

ROSE. Yes but / that's not

HAZEL. It has compromised us. All of this, we have *been compromised* –

ROSE. You don't have a right to electricity.

HAZEL. What a thing to say.

HAZEL starts eating her salad.

ROSE. But you don't.

HAZEL. What a thing to say.

ROSE. Half the developing world exists without it.

HAZEL. Well perhaps they should develop then, / 'scuse me, I'm going to bed.

HAZEL stands, picks up her plate, takes a few slices of bread.

ROBIN. Haze, wait. Just hear her / out at least.

ROSE. We built a nuclear reactor next to the sea then put the emergency generators in the basement! We left them with a shit-show waiting to happen and no evacuation procedure! And then *they* were the ones standing in the dark, trying to fix something we could have predicted, we should have predicted, opening valves by hand, even though it was already too late!

HAZEL. I feel like I should tell you, I'm / sorry but

ROBIN. That's enough.

HAZEL. I never much liked you Rose.

ROBIN. Don't – she's upset, she / doesn't

HAZEL. No, it's true, I always found you sinister, I found your friendship suffocating and sinister and I think the way you speak is affected.

But I hate to waste food, there are starving children in Africa. So there's fruit salad and cream in the fridge for afters, help yourself.

ROBIN. Haze.

HAZEL *leaves the room with her food*. ROBIN *looks at* ROSE.

You're serious aren't you?

ROSE. Might be fun, in some ways. Catch up with the old team.

ROBIN. They didn't like me much.

ROSE. No, of course they didn't. Only two women in the entire plant and you were getting off with both of them.

ROBIN. They didn't know that.

ROSE. Everyone knew that. Hazel knew that.

ROBIN. No.

ROSE. Of course she knew!

ROBIN. No, of course she knew you and I… had, before I met her. But she never suspected that it was still, that we were

ROSE. Ongoing? She did.

ROBIN. No.

ROSE. She did.

ROBIN. I don't know why you'd assume

ROSE. Because she got knocked up, didn't she?

Pause.

ROBIN. No. No, I don't think / that's

ROSE. You don't?

ROBIN. No.

ROSE. Then you're a bloody idiot.

,

ROBIN. Yes. / Maybe, but

ROSE. Because I'm the sort of woman who forgets to take a pill in the morning, I'm just that sort of person, I don't make lists or eat salad, I don't do yoga or – I don't have a pension even.

But Hazel was a very cautious person. I remember when we were on night shifts together, she always – this sounds funny but, she always smelt so lovely. And at first I thought it was you, I thought I was smelling you on her and that was what I found so… but then one day I asked her, what's that lovely smell you always have?

And she said it's suncream.

And I thought, it's January and it's night. And I wondered if maybe she was a bit mentally ill, but I did understand, in that moment, the fundamental difference between Hazel and me, and why you might be more drawn to…

To that sort of woman. To the sort of woman who is cautious, and doesn't make mistakes.

ROBIN. That's not

ROSE. No, it is, so when Lauren happened, I knew it wasn't an accident at all, it was entirely intentional. And I remember, at the time, thinking, it might have been easier Hazel, it might have been easier if you'd just pissed on him.

,

The summer before she was born.
Coming here. Watching you prowl around this table, I prayed, I really prayed that something terrible would happen and she'd lose it.
Lauren.
Don't you think that's wicked?

,

ROBIN. No. I did that too.

ROSE. Did you? You never – that makes me feel a bit. Because it's most awful thing I've ever done. I wished that child ill. With all my heart, and with great

poison

And I think I thought, going away, and time and all that, I think I thought it would numb it a bit. That getting older I'd be a bit more...

Sanguine a bit more philosophical a bit, higher minded.

But now I'm sitting here I'm wondering if it's this room that brings out the worst in me because the thing is, I do genuinely think that what I'm doing, what I'm asking of you is right, but also I realise now, that part of my coming, part of my desire, was to kill her, Hazel.

To put her in a situation where she would be killed.
Where she'd understand, what it is.
To die slowly.

And I'm so ashamed of that. I'm so completely ashamed.

,

ROBIN *reaches for her hand, she moves it away.*

Anyway.

,

ROSE *starts to eat hungrily.*
Through a mouthful, friendly:

Do you like your children?

ROBIN. Yes. Of course.

ROSE. No, only I know quite a few people who don't. They
love them and deeply, but they don't actually like them. And
I know other people who like their children a lot only it's
painfully clear their children don't like them. And you never
wanted them in the first place so I wondered how that went
for you.

ROBIN. I know this sounds callous but. I don't think you could
understand.

ROSE *looks at him, mid-mouthful.*
Nods, swallows.

ROSE. No. I have tried cats. I couldn't be doing with it. People
say it's a substitute but it's not a substitute. I think I am
maternal. Just not towards cats.

,

ROBIN. You never wanted?

ROSE. I never wanted anyone else's. Are you going to eat that?

ROSE *gestures to his plate of salad.*
ROBIN *shakes his head, pushes his plate to* ROSE, *she eats.*
ROSE *remembers suddenly.*

Shit. I told you, didn't I? Idiot.

She rummages in her handbag.
Finds a pill-box, takes one.

ROBIN. What's that?

She swallows it with a drink of water.

ROSE. Birth control. I have to take it with food or it makes me feel sick.

,

ROBIN. So is that still, is that something you have to worry about?

ROSE. What?

ROBIN. You know. Getting. Up the duff.

ROSE *laughs*.

ROSE. I'm sixty-five, Robin.

ROBIN. No I / know, but

ROSE. I mean, even if I did, can you imagine the poor creature? It'd be deformed.

ROBIN. Okay.

ROSE. It would have flippers!

ROBIN. Okay but don't, all I'm asking, it's actually a completely acceptable question, is why is a sixty-five-year old woman taking the fucking pill?

ROSE. Because it annihilates my libido.

,

ROBIN. Does it?

ROSE. Pretty much.

ROBIN. Right.

,

Right. So.

ROSE. It just makes my life a lot easier. Not to want it in the first place.

Pause.
ROSE *keeps eating*.

ROBIN *takes a Peperami out of his pocket.*
Tears it open, breaks it in half and offers her a piece.

What's that?

ROBIN. Peperami. Drove halfway up the motorway for that.

ROSE. Thanks.

ROSE *takes it.*
They both eat.

How are the cows?

ROBIN. Dead.

ROSE *stops eating.*

They were dead when I went back the first time. Couldn't bear to tell Hazel. I told you, she's very sentimental about animals.

ROSE. But you go down there. Every day, morning to night, Hazel said.

ROBIN. I've been digging graves. You need to dig a very big pit for a cow, it takes me a few days just to do one so it's been quite a, quite a slow process.

I have to dig it next to wherever they're lying and then I get the tractor and sort of drag them in.
Then I cover them up and then I conduct a little service.
Say a good poem and sing a good song.

ROSE. Oh, Robbie.

ROBIN. No I sort of... I dunno, I quite enjoy it. I cry a lot. Sometimes I get to the end of a day and I realise I've been crying for... six or seven hours.

ROSE. You must have been very attached to them.

ROBIN. No, not really.

,

She picks up the Geiger counter.
Looks at him, asking for permission.
He nods.

ROSE *runs the Geiger counter over* ROBIN.
It beeps.
She looks at the reading.
She hands it back.

ROSE. It doesn't matter.

I don't want you to think I came because I wanted something
more or I had some sort of, I was harbouring some sort of
hopes because I didn't, I'm not, so. I mean I think I've
grown up a lot. Because I understand, I do understand now,
that for the world not to you know completely fall apart, that
we can't have everything we want just because we want it.

,

She smiles.

I mean, maybe people like you and Hazel can / but

ROBIN. Oh, fuck off. Don't – you can / fuck right off

ROSE. No? Name one thing, in your life, that you wanted and
couldn't have. Something real I mean, not a steak or a…
speedboat

ROBIN. A speedboat?

ROSE. I don't know, you're at that sort of age, one thing.

Pause. ROBIN *thinks. Laughs.*

What?

ROBIN. No, / it's.

ROSE. Tell me.

ROBIN. You'll laugh.

ROSE. Probably.

ROBIN groans.

ROBIN. Fiona.

ROSE laughs.

ROSE. The milkmaid?

ROBIN *shrugs.*
As he talks he clears the plates.

ROBIN. We had this caravan, bottom of the low field, she
rented it off us. I'm walking back from The Ship one night,
cross-country, she's outside in a T-shirt, pair of wellies,
knickers, that's it.

She kissed me back, so she can't have been... I mean it must
have been alright. Not too... necrophiliac. Do you mind if I?

He gestures to ROSE*'s cigarettes.*
She pushes them closer, he takes one.

ROSE. Do you want a light?

ROBIN. No, I just like holding it, her pupils are like Frisbees,
she says 'd'you want one?' I pretend I do, she puts this pill in
my hand, I make a bit of a switcheroo, take one of my blue
ones instead. Which means I've got about half an hour to kill
before lift-off and you know cos it's not like with Hazel, she
just uses the time to put a wash on, so I slow things down a
bit, ask her about her family. But she just shrugs and says
'they live in a cul de sac' then falls asleep in my lap, conks
out, thumb in her mouth. You know and that's alright for a
bit but I've taken this pill and her head's right... there on
ground zero you know and then, then, then I'm terrified
because things are actually starting to happen, and suddenly
I'm on my feet, walking away. The next morning she grins at
me like nothing happened. And I realise she can't, she cannot
possibly imagine, she's designed not to be able to imagine,
how incredibly sad she makes me.

ROBIN *lights the cigarette.*
He smokes.
ROSE *looks at him.*
He does not know he is being watched.

ROSE *crosses her legs.*

*The blackout ends for the day and the electric kettle suddenly
starts to boil.*
The fridge hums.
The oven clock starts to flash.

ROSE *suddenly stands.*
Takes a laptop and charger from her bag.

ROSE. Do you fancy a dance?

ROBIN. What?

ROSE. I just, it's upsetting me. How miserable you look.

ROBIN. Oh, I'm sorry if my existential crisis makes you
uncomfortable.

ROSE. That? That's not a. Oh my God, you think that's a crisis?
You couldn't get it up to shag the milkmaid, it's hardly the
endgame / of your life.

ROBIN. You asked me, so I told you, / so don't

ROSE. No I know, it's just, you just, you used to be so…

She gestures, vaguely, something enormous.

And Hazel, Hazel was so, she was – she used to be a Socialist!

ROBIN. Yes, but she's alright now.

ROSE *makes a face, holds up the lead.*

ROSE. Where can I plug this in?

ROBIN *gestures to a socket.*

ROBIN. But the electricity, we're not supposed / to be

ROSE. This is an emergency.

ROSE *plugs the laptop in and starts it up.*

ROBIN. Hardly.

ROSE. You're having an existential crisis.

ROBIN. Yes, I am, actually, I'm / having a

ROSE. I know, I know, you / feel

ROBIN. I do

ROSE. What?

ROBIN. I feel very

ROSE. What?

,

ROBIN. I feel eroded.

    ROSE *clicks open a programme on her laptop.*

    What are you doing?

ROSE. I'm playing our song.

    She stands, puts her hand out to ROBIN *as a song starts to play from the computer's speakers.*

ROBIN. Oh, God! Do you remember that party? At Douglas's? I wonder if they still have parties like that. Had parties like that.

ROSE. Not the way we did them. Get up.

    ROBIN *laughs, shakes his head.*

ROBIN. I'm enjoying the floor show.

ROSE. Get up you sad old man!

    She drags ROBIN *to his feet, he feigns reluctance, but begins to dance.*
    ROBIN *and* ROSE *dance together.*

    What was the dance?

ROBIN. What dance?

ROSE. You know, the routine.

ROBIN. Oh the

ROSE. Hazel'll know.

ROBIN. Why would Hazel know?

ROSE. Hazel made it up. HAZEL!

ROSE/ROBIN. HAZEL! HAZEL! HAZEL!

HAZEL comes running back in.
She registers the song playing as ROSE *goes to* HAZEL.
Puts her arms around her.

ROSE. I'm sorry. I didn't mean to upset you. Lovely Hazel.

HAZEL. Yes, well. What did you want?

ROSE. You smell lovely, what is it?

HAZEL. What? I don't know, probably just suncream, I don't know what else it would –

ROSE *and* ROBIN *burst out laughing.*
HAZEL *turns to leave.*
ROSE *grabs her hand, pulls her back.*

ROSE. No, wait, play with us!

HAZEL. Grow up, Rose.

ROBIN. How did that dance go?

HAZEL. What dance?

ROBIN. You know, the routine. We did for two hours without stopping that night at Douglas's

ROSE. don't you remember it?

HAZEL. Of course I remember it, I made it up.

ROSE. Yes that's what I – it was like this:

She shows her.

HAZEL. No it wasn't.

ROSE. Something like that / though

HAZEL. No, it wasn't, it's not even – it was like this:

HAZEL does the routine, proficiently.

Standing in a line, they fall into a pretty synchronised routine of a repetitive dance.
The others copying HAZEL, *but growing in confidence and unity as they repeat it.*

They get into their swing.
They grow in confidence and flair.
Even HAZEL *starts to enjoy herself.*

Water starts to seep into the room from under the door to
the bathroom.
It begins to flood the floor.
Presently HAZEL *sees it.*

Rose!

HAZEL *stops dancing.* ROSE *and* ROBIN *continue doing*
the routine.

ROSE. What?

HAZEL. What's the matter with you, I asked you, three / times
I asked you

ROBIN. Okay, Haze, calm down

HAZEL. I will not calm down, don't tell me to

ROBIN. It's just a bit of / water

HAZEL. You're pathetic, you know that? I feel sorry for you,
I really do, I'm sorry you've had such a, that your life's been
so, because, but that isn't our fault. It isn't our fault and it's
embarrassing, actually, honestly, it's really, you've
embarrassed yourself coming here like this, so well done

ROBIN *stops dancing.* ROSE *continues to dance.*

ROBIN. That's *enough*

HAZEL. well done you silly bitch

ROBIN. HAZEL!

HAZEL. you know what she's done, don't you?

ROBIN. Yes, / but

HAZEL. You know what she's / done to us?

ROBIN. I'm just saying, / there's no need to

HAZEL. SHE SHAT IN OUR TOILET! YOU SHAT IN OUR TOILET ROSE, WHAT HAVE YOU GOT TO SAY FOR YOURSELF?

ROSE stops dancing and kisses ROBIN on the mouth.
HAZEL stares at them.
The water is halfway across the floor now.
They part.
Pause.
HAZEL walks towards ROSE.
HAZEL turns towards ROBIN and slaps him.
ROBIN laughs.
It turns into a cough.
Some blood comes from his mouth.

He stops laughing.
He reaches for HAZEL.

ROBIN. Oh, bloody hell… Hazel.

HAZEL. I'm here. I'm here. Oh my. Robin.

He tries to wipe it away, embarrassed.
ROSE watches him cling to HAZEL.

ROBIN. It's alright. Could I have a tea towel please?

HAZEL gives him a tea towel, he wipes his mouth.

HAZEL. Is this – are you?

ROBIN. It's nothing. I'm sorry.

HAZEL rubs his back.

HAZEL. It's alright, shhhh, can you cough it all up? You'll feel better if you can cough it all up.

ROBIN coughs some more.
Tries to wipe his mouth, speaks through it.

ROBIN. It'll stop in a minute.

HAZEL. Has this, this has, it's happened before has it?

ROBIN. Not really.

HAZEL. Not really? Not really, oh my God oh / my my my my darling

ROBIN. A few times. It passes.

HAZEL. I asked you not to go down there, I begged / you

ROBIN. I know.

HAZEL. This would never have happened if you'd / just

ROBIN. I know!

HAZEL. Well good. I'm glad you know, I'm glad you can admit that. I'm sorry. I'm so, I don't know why I said that, that was a horrible thing to, how do you feel?

ROBIN. Bit rough.

HAZEL. Right. Right well you probably just need a good night's sleep.

ROBIN *wipes the blood from his chin.*

ROBIN. Yes.

HAZEL. I don't know. I don't know what to, do you want me to call an ambulance?

ROBIN *shakes his head and sits down.*
If the song has not already finished, ROBIN *now shuts the laptop.*

ROBIN. I'm going.

HAZEL. What?

ROBIN. I'm going to the power station.

HAZEL. Don't be stupid. You should be in a hospital.

ROBIN. No thank you.

HAZEL. What?

ROBIN. I said no thank you.

HAZEL. Robin.

ROBIN. My God aren't you sick of thinking about your fucking
    body all the time? It's just meat, it's rented meat who gives a
    shit. We used to wrestle the atom all night on a crisp sandwich.

HAZEL. Yes well you can do it when you're young but you're
    sick, you're really sick and if we don't get you some help,
    you'll die Robin, do you understand me? I don't know
    why I'm treating / it like a discussion, it's not a discussion

ROBIN. Yes but I've been thinking about that and / the thing is

HAZEL. I'm going to call an / ambulance.

ROBIN. the thing is I'd quite like to die at some point.

HAZEL. Take that back! Take it back!

ROBIN. No.

    One day the world will be full of billions of beautifully kept
    little machines living forever and we'll all want to kill
    ourselves anyway we're so bored.

HAZEL. Take it back. Robin. Please.

    ,

    Please.

    He shakes his head.
    She starts to cry.
    He pulls her on to his lap or close to him.
    He holds her.
    Tender.
    She clings to him.
    He comforts her like a child.
    ROSE *watches them from a distance.*
    Tries to look like she isn't.

ROBIN. Come on Haze. It's just a little bit of blood. It's just
    like... what's that show the kids used to... the crystal
    whatsit, fucking shite, / they loved it

HAZEL. The Crystal Maze

ROBIN. the Crystal Maze, exactly, and that's it, all it is, is now there's just a little clock counting down in the corner of the screen and there's a bald fellow outside the door playing the harmonica. You know, and that's. Alarming, but. I've always been better with a deadline. You know that.

HAZEL. And what about me. What about what I, the things that I

ROBIN. What is it, Lauren?

HAZEL. of course Lauren. Always Lauren.

ROBIN. Because you know a hundred years ago you'd probably be in the ground by now.
Dead from… Flu, or an ear infection… childbirth even, but because of science, and because we've decided that natural decay is unnatural, and because of the distance the human brain has travelled us, forcing our bodies to keep up, here you are, alive and kicking and that's of course, you know, marvellous, but you're a terrifying act to follow my darling, do you know that? You are, and so, when I want to shake her, Lauren I mean, when I feel like attaching a pair of jump leads to her fucking ears, I remind myself of that, that her mother is a giantess (a pain in the arse, also, true) and but d'you know what I think? I think the only thing that will force Lauren to grow is for her to wake up one day and find that we're not there any more, and I know what you're about to say, you'll say you're her mother, and you'll want to talk about duty, but what I think, what I honestly think is this is your duty, you have a real duty to that child, to fuck off at some point.

Pause.

HAZEL. But… but what, um… what about the cows?

ROBIN. The cows are dead my love. I'm going to pack a bag.

ROBIN *goes out.* HAZEL *looks at* ROSE.
ROSE *gets her cigarettes and walks towards the door.*
HAZEL *grabs her by the hair and pulls her back.*
It comes off in her hand.

HAZEL. Rose. What.

ROSE. It's fine, it was a while ago, I'm fine now. It's just it takes forever for it to grow back. Specially at our age.

ROSE *fixes her wig.*

Do you want to call your children?

HAZEL. Why?

ROSE. To let them know your plans.

HAZEL. What plans? I haven't said anything, I haven't got any… plans, what plans?

,

Is that what people do? Is that what the others did?

ROSE. Some of them. The others are waiting till they get there because otherwise it gets a bit, they get emotional, don't they, children? Douglas's daughter, oh God, we had a time of it there. She spat in my face. Crying, lying on the floor, 'you can't take him, it's not fair, I'm not ready' all that jazz.

ROSE *laughs.*

They don't like having things taken away from them.

HAZEL. But… but you're doing it for them. That's why you're doing it.

ROSE. No I know, it's funny, isn't it?

Maybe you'd prefer Robin to call them, / or

HAZEL. I haven't said – stop – rushing me!

Pause.

ROSE. You don't have to worry. I won't. I won't go near him.

HAZEL. Oh, okay then.

ROSE. No, I know, I wouldn't believe me either. But it's true.

I went to a therapist once, in America, she said to me, 'Rose, are you familiar with the definition of madness as doing the same thing over and over and expecting the result to be different?'

I said No. But ask me again.

HAZEL *laughs*. ROSE *laughs*.

Do you think Lauren's going to be alright?

HAZEL. I don't know. She's thirty-eight and she thinks she's still young.

You're lucky, you've always had a good head shape. I'd look like an egg.

Where was it?

ROSE *touches her breast*.
HAZEL *nods*.

I used to be so jealous of your chest.
You used to say 'oh but the backache is terrible' and I wanted to smash your face into the table.

Did they take both?

ROSE. Yes.

Pause.

HAZEL. I want a cup of tea, do you want a cup of tea?

ROSE. Sure, go on.

HAZEL *reboils the kettle and makes tea*.

I'm sorry about the bathroom.

HAZEL. That's alright. Milk?

ROSE. No / thank you.

HAZEL. No, you said –

ROSE. I'm not allowed. Dairy promotes cell production.

HAZEL. Does it?

ROSE. That's why we give milk to babies.

HAZEL. I never knew that.

ROSE. No well why would you? You're not a doctor.

HAZEL. No.

ROSE. You're not a biologist.

HAZEL. No.

ROSE. You're a physicist.

,

HAZEL. Retired.

ROSE. Yes / but

HAZEL. I know what you're doing. It's not, it isn't…

Why do you even want me there?

Pause.

ROSE. It'll sound silly but.

You were who I wanted to be when I grew up. I thought, one day I'll be like Hazel.

I won't smoke cigarettes and I'll wear suncream and plan the week's meals ahead and get a slow cooker and not just buy sandwiches from petrol stations and I'll keep the bathroom really clean not just give it a wipe when people are coming over and I'll stop crying all the time and I'll do exercise and have a really neat handbag and do washing regularly not just when I've run out of knickers and stop losing earrings and not stay awake reading till four in the morning and feel like shit the next day and I'll find out how tracker mortgages work and be fifteen minutes early to everything and most of all most of all I'll know when I've had enough.

But I never quite got there. And I think it's a bit late now. And then tonight I saw your washing outside, on the line, and I thought about you, pegging it out, and how many times in your life you'd done that and no one noticed.

And I thought, that woman holds up the world.

So that's why, really.

,

HAZEL. We're an island.

,

ROSE. Well –

HAZEL. No, I mean literally, we're a very coastal country. We've got miles and miles of coast, and it's windy. Why aren't they thinking about wave power? That's what they should be thinking about.

Pause.

Douglas has got a daughter has he?

ROSE. Yes.

HAZEL. And so he's married, or?

ROSE. Um, widowed I / think.

HAZEL. Widowed, really? That's, poor Douglas.

Pause.

When you go, I'd take some mugs. For teas and coffees. Never enough mugs in that staffroom, used to drive me crazy.

,

And teaspoons. No one ever thinks about teaspoons.

Pause.

Or tea towels, has he still got that tattoo?

ROSE. Who, Douglas?

HAZEL. Yes, on his arm, a tree with bare branches, he added a leaf every year.

ROSE. I don't know. I didn't see his arms, he was wearing a, it was a sort of um, running top?

HAZEL. Oh, so he's still keeping fit then. Good for him.

,

no, good for him.

,

I've got some tea towels you can take actually, if you…

HAZEL *gets up and collects some tea towels, mugs and teaspoons into a bag.*

Whatever happens, I'm not sure I can stay here any more, to be honest. It feels foul to me.

Pause.

I can't give you the car, it belongs to the insurance company. How did you get here?

ROSE. I came in a / taxi.

HAZEL. A taxi, that's right, you said.

Pause.
Then HAZEL *goes out.*
She returns with the phone, dials, waits.
Presently the call is connected.

Hello, Denny? It's Hazel.

,

Hello love, we'd like a taxi please. In an hour, do you think you can –

,

Half-past, that's fine, thank you, from the cottage, yes.

,

To the power station.

,

The power station, yes

,

Well to the edge of the exclusion zone then.

,

Robin and a a a a friend of ours.

,

I might do.

,

HAZEL *adds teabags and a jar of instant coffee to the bag of mugs and tea towels. Maybe some milk.*

I said I might do, I haven't decided yet.

,

I know.

,

I know. I'll pay you fifty pounds extra.

,

A hundred then.

,

Not in cash, I haven't got a hundred quid in cash just in my –

(*Hand over the phone, to* ROSE.) Have you –

ROSE *shakes her head.*

(*Back to* DENNY.) No, you'll have to stop at the Co-op then.

,

Is it? Well there's one outside the post office then.

,

No, they won't need picking up again.

Thank you Denny. Half-past. Yes, just sound the horn. We'll come out. Thank you – sorry, Denny – how's the little one today?

,

Is she?

Oh dear, yes that is a bit worrying isn't it?
Tell Maria not to fret.
Two of mine went through the same thing.
Hm. Cayenne pepper. Dab it around the nostrils. Helps it clot.

,

You too pet. Bye now.

HAZEL *hangs up. Pause.*

I'd better come with you to the cash point at least. Denny's
a very nice man but he takes the piss sometimes.

,

Rose. I'm frightened.

ROSE. That's alright.

HAZEL. It's just it's very hard to, I don't know / how to

ROSE. I know

HAZEL. I don't know how to want less.

The phone rings, it makes them both jump.
HAZEL *answers it.*

Hello?

,

Oh, hello darling. Are you –

HAZEL *becomes afraid she is going to cry.*

Hang on sweetheart, Dad wants to talk to you – ROBIN!
ROBIN! What did you do about the washing machine in
the end?

,

Oh dear, yes you do have to activate them or they won't –

ROBIN *enters.*

It's Lauren – you speak to her – your father's got something
to tell you sweetheart.

She holds the phone out.
He stares at her, shakes his head.

Please. I can't.

Eventually, ROBIN *takes the phone.*

ROBIN. Hi Loz…

He sees ROSE *watching him.*

Just a second piccalilli, just going to take you upstairs…

He takes the phone out, closes the door behind him.
Perhaps we hear the rumble of his voice from upstairs as he
talks to LAUREN.
The women listen to it.
ROSE *tries to comfort* HAZEL, *she smacks her away.*

HAZEL. Don't touch me.

Pause.
HAZEL *gathers herself and abruptly stands up.*

Sorry. Sorry, d'you mind if I?

ROSE. Whatever you / need to

HAZEL. Just, I have my routine. It's later than I thought, if
    I don't do it now, it won't get done, and I'll feel it tomorrow.

ROSE. You don't mind me sitting here while / you

HAZEL. No, that's fine. I'll just pretend you're not there.

HAZEL finds her yoga mat and rolls it out on a dry patch of
the floor.
ROSE watches her.
HAZEL kicks off her shoes and takes up her position.
She starts to stretch, a warm-up.
ROSE goes to the door, opens it, takes out her cigarettes.
The sound of the sea rushes in from the dark.

ROSE. I did hear the bells you know
    From the church, under the water.

I heard them as clear as anything, ringing out across the
shingle and I thought about them all, going in for evening
prayers, till the tide came in and the sea went black and
I felt the water was round my ankles.

She looks at HAZEL.
She puts her cigarettes down.
She kicks off her own shoes and takes up position adjacent
to HAZEL.
ROSE *taking her lead from* HAZEL, *the two women perform*
a yoga routine.

ROBIN *enters with a bag, watches from the doorway for*
a moment.
He finds a pair of yellow washing-up gloves, puts them on.
He sees ROSE'*s cigarettes on the table.*
He takes one, goes to the open door, lights up.
He gets a broom or a mop and starts sweeping the water out
of the door, smoking as he does.
The women repeat their routine as the lights slowly fade.

Through the open door
the sound of the sea and waves breaking
mixes with the movement of ROBIN'*s broom*
and the women
as they try to keep breathing.

Out of this, very gradually, the sound of a wave building.
It grows and grows
It crashes upon us.
Silence.

Distantly, a church bell rings.
As if from under the water.
The sound distorted but unmistakable.
End.

Lucy Kirkwood is a British playwright and screenwriter whose plays include: *The Children* (Royal Court Theatre, 2016); *Chimerica* (Almeida Theatre and West End, 2013; winner of the 2014 Olivier Award for Best New Play, the 2013 Evening Standard Best Play Award, the 2014 Critics' Circle Best New Play Award, and the Susan Smith Blackburn Prize); *NSFW* (Royal Court, 2012); *small hours* (co-written with Ed Hime; Hampstead Theatre, 2011); *Beauty and the Beast* (with Katie Mitchell; National Theatre, 2010); *Bloody Wimmin*, as part of *Women, Power and Politics* (Tricycle Theatre, 2010); *it felt empty when the heart went at first but it is alright now* (Clean Break and Arcola Theatre, 2009; winner of the 2012 John Whiting Award); *Hedda* (Gate Theatre, 2008); and *Tinderbox* (Bush Theatre, 2008). She won the inaugural Berwin Lee UK Playwrights Award in 2013.